A Student's  packed with ... ...learn to think Christianly about gender, social media, and more. And yet it's short, easy to read, and biblically sound. I wish every young person would read this and discuss it with a caring adult.

Sean McDowell
Professor of Christian Apologetics, Biola University,
La Mirada, California
Best-selling author and popular speaker

Our gospel glasses have become so muddied by 'what's right by the world' that we struggle to see cultural issues clearly through the lens of Biblical truth. For this reason, I wish I could put this book in the hands of every Christian teenager, and adult too for that matter. In a winsome, easy-to-follow way, Walt guides us in learning to rethink the cultural narrative so we walk in step with God's Word.

Kristen Hatton
Author of *The Gospel-Centered Life in Exodus for Students, Face Time: Your Identity in a Selfie World* and *Get Your Story Straight*

What makes Walt Mueller such an important resource for youth workers is that he's a keen student of both the culture and the Word. And he puts both of those tools to good use in this little book. The book is readable, biblical, and, of course, up-to-the-minute relevant. I especially appreciate that Walt opts in this book to move beyond vague and safe 'lessons', and invites students to look through his 'World, Word, Walk' lens to think about two of the toughest, hot-button topics in adolescent culture: social media and gender identity. I could imagine a tool like this being used by a discipleship group as a discussion guide, or an individual student who truly wants to take discipleship seriously, or a youth worker who's looking for deeper ways to engage hard topics. I enthusiastically recommend it!

Duffy Robbins
Professor of Christian Ministries, Grove City
College, Grove City, Pennsylvania

Books on culture have a way of becoming obsolete before the ink dries. In a rapidly morphing cultural landscape it feels like it's impossible to keep up with the latest trends. That's what makes this book so important. In *Navigating Culture* Walt gives us a practical and relevant toolkit for engaging the culture in which we live, parent and do our ministry. Instead of weighing in on the latest social media sensations or most recent media offerings, Walt gives us a 'map' that remains useful even when the specific cultural artefacts are constantly changing. This book contains the wisdom of someone who has navigated culture for decades on behalf of parents and leaders everywhere, and gives us access to the basic tools we will need to find our own way, and guide next generations through the complexity of what post-modern, post-Christian, post-truth culture throws at us. A must-read resource for anyone who loves teenagers.

Marv Penner
Director, All About Youth and the National Center for Excellence in Youth Ministry
Speaker and author of several books, including
Help! My Kids Are Hurting

Walt Mueller is the preeminent guide to culture for parents, youth workers, and teachers. Culture is the water that our students are swimming in every single day, and Walt has taught me over the years how to navigate our ever changing culture for myself and my students. I'm so grateful for this insightful and easily digestible book that will give you the foundations you need to have rich conversations concerning how we should be thinking biblically about complex topics like gender and social media. Whether you're a parent or youth worker, read this book and use the included discussions with your students to help you reflect and engage on these important topics.

Kevin Yi
College and Young Adults Pastor, Church Everyday and video producer for Rooted Ministry

This is a must-read for any parent and youth worker who cares about kids and culture. The stakes are too high and there's just too much to navigate in today's culture without a helpful guide who is seasoned with cultural wisdom and biblical knowledge. Thankfully, Walt is that guide who can lead parents, youth workers and teenagers to travel life well. It's a fabulous resource!

Doug Fields
Youth Pastor & Co-founder of Downloadyouthministry.com

Walt Mueller, one of the most trusted voices in 'cultural exegesis,' has written a clear and accessible primer on what it means to live

Christianly in our current world. He uses simple metaphors to unpack complex ideas in ways that are relatable and relevant. While directly addressing two of the most pressing cultural issues facing all teenagers—gender and social media—this slim volume offers important wisdom and truth that can be used to think Christianly about a host of cultural realities. Get this book for your kids, students, and teens. But first read it yourself — because we all have things to learn and progress to make when it comes to living Christianly.

Crystal Kirgiss
Author, speaker and teacher, Purdue University,
West Lafayette, Indiana
Young Life VP of Discipleship

Young people are watching and listening to a cultural narrative – one that is weaving before them a system of values, morals, and beliefs. As Walt points out, our kids are marinating in a secular culture and they are often doing it without any biblical guidance. We must choose to be a stronger, more convincing, Christ-centered voice to our young people. This is a must-read.

Julie E. Lowe
Counselor and Faculty Member, CCEF

This book challenges teenagers not to run away from, but to run into the hard questions they face today by offering biblical answers and theological conviction. It is a brave new world—here you will find the wisdom and courage you need to navigate it.

Stephen J. Nichols
Author of *R. C. Sproul: A life*
President, Reformation Bible College, CAO
Ligonier Ministries, Sanford, Florida

TRACK CULTURE

A STUDENT'S GUIDE TO **NAVIGATING CULTURE**

WALT
MUELLER

SERIES EDITED BY
JOHN PERRITT

CHRISTIAN
FOCUS

tym

Scripture quotations are from *The Holy Bible, English Standard Version*, copyright © 2001 by Crossway Bibles, a publishing ministry of Good News Publishers. Used by permission. All rights reserved. ESV Text Edition: 2011.

Copyright © Walt Mueller 2021

paperback ISBN 978-1-5271-0694-9
ebook ISBN 978-1-5271-0781-6

10 9 8 7 6 5 4 3 2 1

First published in 2021
by
Christian Focus Publications Ltd,
Geanies House, Fearn, Ross-shire,
IV20 1TW, Great Britain

www.christianfocus.com

with

Reformed Youth Ministries,
1445 Rio Road East
Suite 201D
Charlottesville,
Virginia, 22911

Cover by MOOSE77

Printed by Page Bros, Norwich

CONTENTS

Series Introduction

Christianity is a religion of words, because our God is a God of words. He created through words, calls Himself the Living Word, and wrote a book (filled with words) to communicate to His children. In light of this, pastors and parents should take great efforts to train the next generation to be readers. *Track* is a series designed to do exactly that.

Written for students, the *Track* series addresses a host of topics in three primary areas: Doctrine, Culture, and the Christian Life. *Track's* booklets are theologically rich, yet accessible. They seek to engage and challenge the student without dumbing things down.

One definition of a track reads: *a way that has been formed by someone else's footsteps.* The goal of the *Track* series is to point us to that 'someone else'—Jesus Christ. The One who forged a track to guide His followers. While we cannot follow this track perfectly, by His grace and Spirit He calls us to strive to stay on the path. It is our prayer that this series of booklets would help guide Christ's Church until He returns.

In His Service,

John Perritt
RYM's Director of Resources
Series Editor

Introduction

It was a boring Saturday afternoon in the middle of summer. I was eleven years old. My buddy Mike and I were looking for something to do. One of us decided it might be fun to walk a couple of miles to the local shopping center. We had absolutely no idea why we were going to go there except that we had never walked that far before and there was a certain sense of unknown adventure attached to getting out of our neighborhood without our parents knowing that we were doing something they would have surely forbidden. Bad decision #1 was overstepping our boundaries.

About a mile into our walk, we realized that it was taking us a bit longer than we expected. In an effort to get there more quickly, I stopped walking, turned around to face oncoming traffic, and threw out my thumb. Yeah... an eleven-year-old hitch-hiking...which was something I had never done before. I had no regard for our safety. I just wanted to get there quickly. Bad decision #2 was risking putting ourselves at the mercy of creepers. The good news is that in spite of this second bad decision, everything turned out OK. In fact, the first approaching car slowed down and came to a stop. A woman as old as my grandmother rolled down the window in her big luxury sedan and told us to get in. Once we were in she angrily reprimanded us by saying, 'What the heck are you boys doing hitch-hiking???' When we got to the store she looked at us and barked, 'GET OUT! And don't ever let me catch you hitch-hiking again!'

Bad decision #3 is the one that's stuck with me the longest. When we got to the shopping center, we realized we had no money. Long story short, our trip now needed a purpose of some kind, so we decided to hit the pay-by-the-pound candy bins at the large grocery store. Of course, it was a decision we made after a bit of discussion, a discussion which ended with us both agreeing that stealing is something that people do all the time. Mike filled his pockets and walked out of the crowded store undetected. I nervously grabbed and pocketed one small piece of candy and followed.

You might expect me to finish the story by telling you how we were caught by the manager, were picked up by the police, and sent to a juvenile detention center. That didn't happen. Instead, with each step taken on our way home, our guilt increased and we knew that when faced with this choice, we had chosen wrongly. Bad decision. Eventually, we turned around and went back to the store...walking this time. And just as we had sneaked the candy out, we now snuck it back in as a way to assuage our guilt. In hindsight we should have probably confessed to the store manager, but we didn't. Still, there were powerful lessons learned.

Here's something to consider: While you might read this story and agree that 11-year-old Walt made bad decisions, there are others in this world who might not think it was that big a deal. What I look back on and label as 'wrong', others might say was 'nothing wrong.' Well, who's right? It all depends on who you've listened to as the authority in your life. Some people choose to follow the path of their own personal preferences and feelings. Others listen to the voices that raised them, telling them what to believe. Others go with the flow of their friends.

When it comes to determining the path of your life in the everyday matters of life, what authority will you follow?

Choices always have outcomes and consequences. And the choices we make are influenced by the voices we choose to follow. Who will we allow to shape our beliefs, behaviors, and decisions? In today's world, the voices around us are many and conflicting. When we finally become serious about our faith, we now are faced with choosing to listen either to God's Word—the Bible—or to the world. I'll be the first to admit, it's a struggle.

This is a little book that's ultimately about the voices we choose to follow and the choices we then make. My hope is that just as my little 11-year-old self had a Saturday-afternoon moment learning a lesson about voices and choices, this book will help shape your daily decision-making for the rest of your life, as you learn practical skills that will help you follow the voice of Jesus in the midst of a culture that all too often points you in a variety of other directions.

It's my hope that while you might wind up reading this book alone, you'll talk about it with others who will be reading it too. Just as there's strength in numbers when it comes to making bad decisions, there's strength in numbers when brothers and sisters in Christ, young and old together, support and encourage each other to live counter-culturally to the glory of God, while living in a culture that is all too often very good at convincing us to live counter to the Gospel. Read and discuss this little book with your parents, your youth worker, and your youth group peers. Then, work to put the principles and strategies into action.

1. Soup and Sandwiches

Have you ever argued with someone about sandwiches? I have…way too many times. It all started when I was eighteen years old and I left my hometown in the Philadelphia suburbs and moved just 300 miles west to attend college outside of Pittsburgh. I quickly realized that even though I was still living in my home state of Pennsylvania, I had actually moved to what seemed like another planet…and that's where the sandwich comes in.

If I were to show you around Philadelphia there are lots of things I'd want you to experience…especially the food! One of those delicacies is a local sandwich that I once naively thought everyone called a 'hoagie.' Then I moved to Pittsburgh. I asked a new-found classmate from the area where I could get one of my beloved hoagies. He looked at me like I was speaking another language. To him, I was.

'Umm...what's a hoagie?', he asked through a facial expression that told me he thought I was nuts. 'Umm...it's a sandwich on a long roll that's filled with meat, cheese, lettuce, tomato, onions, oil, and vinegar. Duh,' I replied. His eyes lit up, 'Oh, you mean a sub?' Now it was my turn: 'A sub?!? No, I mean a hoagie!' That's when the sandwich arguments began. And as I've traveled around the country I've had to continue to argue as I've encountered people who have misnamed my hoagie all kinds of things, including 'Grinder', 'Wedge', 'Hero', 'Po' Boy', 'Spuckie', 'Torpedo', 'Gondola', and who knows what else.

The reality is that nobody in these sandwich wars of mine was wrong. Rather, we were all being true to the unique local *culture* of our different hometowns. Our 'sandwich wars' were only the tip of the iceberg regarding the marked differences in how we understood life and how we lived it. (Don't even ask me about our arguments over whether or not to call Coca-Cola 'soda' or 'pop'...which may both be wrong if you're a 'Coke' drinker from the South!)

Whether you know it or not, from the moment you were born you have been part of a culture. And, as is the case for me, your particular culture has shaped and influenced you in ways you're not even aware of. And, as you will come to see as we travel this little journey together, God has much to say about culture. But before we get to God's order, design, plans, and desires for culture, we need to define *culture*.

WHAT IS CULTURE?

Culture, it has been said, is one of the most difficult words in the English language to define. Take time to Google 'culture', and you will find yourself falling into a never-ending rabbit hole filled with endless definitions. Let me try to make it easy for you with a couple of definitions of culture that have been helpful to me.

A Godly thinker and Christian leader by the name of John Stott defines culture as 'a tapestry, intricate and often beautiful, which is woven together by a given society to express its corporate identity.'[1] According to this definition, the tapestry of my world included a sandwich known as a hoagie. Depending on where you are from, the tapestry of your

---

1   John Stott, *The Lausanne Covenant* (Minneapolis: World Wide Publications, 1975), p.26.

culture probably calls it something else. But our tapestries aren't completely different. While there are unique local threads in each, our local cultures share many of the same threads since we are all part of an even larger western culture where people tend to think in generally the same way about the bigger issues of life. For example, we are all shaped similarly by living under similar governmental systems, watching the same movies and television, and being marketed the same clothing styles.

My friend Bill Romanowski has spent his life looking at the life-shaping cultural messages you and I see and hear every day in our favorite music, films, television, books, and online world. He says that culture refers to 'the way humans define and live in God's world.' It is a collection of 'ideals and beliefs, values and assumptions, that makes up a kind of master plan for living and interpreting life.'[2]

CULTURE IS A SOUP

Let's think of culture as including what we believe, what we do, and how we live our lives day to day. Because we share our culture with others, it binds us together with those

---

2   William D. Romanowski, *Eyes Wide Open* (Grand Rapids: Brazos, 2007), pp. 44, 49.

who think and live in a similar manner. I like to think of my culture as 'the soup' of beliefs and behaviors that I swim in every day. My cultural soup shapes how I think about identity, relationships, sex, life purpose, gender, justice, work, play, academics, money, race, authority, and everything else under the sun. Because this is where I live, soak, and marinate 24/7, there are ideas I adopt without even thinking about them (for example, a long sandwich is a hoagie), and there are things I do based on the fact that I have adopted those ideas (for example, argue about sandwich names with those who have grown up in a different 'sandwich culture'!).

I've learned over the years that everyone swims in culture. Wherever there are people, there is culture. I've also learned that culture exercises more power over all of us than we know or are willing to admit.

Have you ever spent an entire hot summer day in a swimming pool? You just can't get enough. And when the afternoon finally comes to an end and you have to climb out of the water to head home for dinner, the effects of your time in the pool are obvious. You are dripping wet. The chlorine has left your eyes red. Your head might feel a little water-logged and stuffy. And your fingertips are all shriveled up. Your time in the pool actually *changed* you in a variety of ways. Culture has that same effect. It changes us. It shapes us. It forms us. And if we are not careful, it will even deform and misshape us by pushing us away from God's good desires for who we are and how we are to live in our world.

WHAT MAP WILL YOU FOLLOW?

You need to realize that the cultural soup you swim in each and every day *is* changing and shaping you. New ingredients (music, film, websites, ideas) are being poured into the soup each and every day. What you read, what you listen to, what you watch, how you spend your time, who you spend time with…all those things make up the 'soup' that maps out for you a path through life, guiding you into what to believe and how to behave. This is why it's so important for you to understand the particular cultural soup you're swimming in and the role it plays in your life. You see, when Jesus Christ calls us to 'come and follow me,' He is inviting us into a life where He guides us through His Word, the Bible, into an understanding of what to believe and how to behave. His purpose in doing so is to lead us into a life where we are able to flourish and grow into the fullness of all He has in store for us, not only on this earth, but for all eternity!

We need to be intent on following God's map for our lives rather than the cultural map for our lives. Sure, there will be times when the cultural map will get it right and agree with God's map. But more often than not, those two maps will lead in different directions. Jesus tells us that there is a wide and easy way through life, but that wide and easy well-traveled way leads to destruction. He maps out a way for us to live that is narrow and difficult, but that is the way that leads to life (Matt. 7:13-14).

IN OR OUT OF THE POOL?

Think again about summertime swimming in the local pool. I've watched the lifeguards and caretakers at public pools regularly test the water. They skim it to remove anything they spot in the water that shouldn't be in the water. They treat the water with chemicals, testing it regularly throughout the day to be sure that it remains clean and the way it's supposed to be. As long as the culture of the water tests clean, the lifeguards allow us to stay in the pool. But if a test shows something unhealthy in the water, whistles are blown and everyone is told to get out. Each and every summer, I see multiple news reports on pools shutting down because of the presence of a bacteria known as fecal coliform. Just the word 'fecal' should cause us to take notice and realize that this is *not* the kind of water in which to be swimming, because it might somehow compromise our health in dangerous ways! The pool might close for a few hours, a couple of days, or in extreme cases for a week at a time because the culture of the water is not the way it's supposed to be. While we might not be able to see the dangers lurking in the water, they are there. And while it might *feel* okay to be swimming in the midst of the invisible dangers, swimming in them means that we are risking compromising our health. Why? Because without even knowing it, what's in the water has an effect on us.

So, what actually is the effect that culture has on us? Keep reading!

Main Point

Culture is not optional. It's an ever-present 'map for life' that either shapes or misshapes our beliefs and behaviors.

Questions for Reflection

- What are some aspects of your culture that are unique and different from other cultures? (foods, words, beliefs, behaviors, clothing, etc.)

- How have you seen culture misshape or deform people in your generation?

- Where do you see today's culture agreeing with the map of God's Word? Disagreeing with the map of God's Word?

2. We all Wear Glasses

I recently watched a video describing the eyesight challenges faced by people living in sub-Saharan Africa. Like many of us living here in the United States, some had battled poor eyesight from as early as childhood. Others could see, but couldn't focus well enough to be able to read. Many had contracted eye diseases and disorders that limited their vision to the point where they had trouble navigating even the easiest and most normal daily life tasks. But unlike us, getting to an eye doctor is a virtual impossibility for these people. In fact, in sub-Saharan Africa, the ratio of optometrists to people is about 1 to every 8 million! Imagine what it's like for those with poor eyesight who finally do get to visit an eye doctor to have their vision checked and then corrected with the proper prescription. Watching videos of the wonder and awe these people experience is amazing! They put on glasses and have an 'Aha!' moment where they can see clearly for the first time!

I know that some of you wear contact lenses or glasses in order to overcome deficiencies in your eyesight. You, like me, know what it's like to take out your contacts or remove your glasses, only to be looking at everything in a blur. You can't read. Maybe you can't make out faces. The pictures on your smartphones are unclear. You have difficulty seeing the baseball when it's pitched. Driving is a dangerous endeavor. But then in that space that exists between your face and everything in the outside world you place the correctly-prescribed lenses, and suddenly it all comes into focus with amazing clarity!

Thinking about our eyesight offers a helpful way to think about the way that culture shapes our lives. The cultural soup that we swim in every hour of every day has an effect on the way we look at the world.

WHAT GLASSES ARE YOU WEARING?

I like to think of it this way, we all wear 'glasses' that shape the way we look at everything in the world around us. Take for example the issue of identity. Experts tell us that as teenagers, we are working to figure out who we are and to find our place in the world. If I look at the issue of identity through the set of glasses 'prescribed' by the current cultural soup, I will most likely come to believe that my identity is to be found in a variety of things, including what I look like and/or my achievements (grades, championships, awards, etc.). Having internalized this understanding of identity, many of our peers do everything they can to create a persona on social media that aspires to something way beyond the reality of who they *actually* are or ever *could* be. Ultimately, as most of us painfully know through our own experience, this leads to great stress and anxiety.

The glasses we choose to put on and look *through* shape...or even misshape...the way we look at everything in the world. Culture has power! This is why we need to think about the concept of a *worldview*.

Think for a minute about your current music playlist. The music you and I listen to is all part—just one small part—of our cultural soup. But along with every other cultural ingredient that we swim in, our music refines and tweaks the prescription for the glasses we choose to wear. You see, all popular music communicates a worldview. The messages communicated lyrically and visually make both overt and covert suggestions on how to think, talk, act, and live. Certain values and beliefs are promoted as virtuous. Others are portrayed negatively. What we listen to and watch shapes us, sometimes without us even knowing it.

WHAT'S A WORLDVIEW?

Whether you know it or not, every one of us has a worldview. It's the model, lens, framework and basic beliefs through which we view the world around us, our purpose in life, and our future. That's right...we all wear worldview glasses!

What does a worldview do? Bill Romanowski says that our worldview maps out life for us as it 'describes the way the world is, while also providing a model for the way the world ought to be.'[1]

Shaped mostly by culture from the day you were born, your worldview gives you answers—whether you've thought about them consciously or unconsciously—to not only the

---

1   Romanowski, *Eyes Wide Open*, p.59.

identity question, but to all the questions you have about life, including:

- Where am I?
- Who's in control?
- Who am I?
- Why am I here?
- What's wrong with the world?
- How can I know right from wrong?
- What is right and what is wrong?
- What should I believe about academics, work, sexuality, gender, family, etc.?
- What's the remedy for what's wrong with this world?

Each of us lives our culturally-influenced worldview every day. It's the basis for how we think and act. Some of us have consciously chosen our worldview. For others...most of us perhaps...our worldview is an unconscious collection of answers we've picked up along the way as we've been swimming in the soup of our culture. For example, all of our music, film, books, advertisements, etc. communicate something to us about what to believe and how to live in this world. This is why it is so important that each of us take the time to understand culture, what it is, how it functions, and how it is influencing us all...without us even knowing it.

The worldview 'glasses' you choose to wear will shape how you understand, interpret, and live your life. It is shaping your decisions about identity, relationships, sex, gender, justice, work, play, academics, money, race, authority, and everything else under the sun. If you're wearing the wrong prescription, your worldview 'glasses' will keep you from understanding how the way things in life really are, and how they should be. You will consistently have difficulty seeing clearly and finding your way. In fact, you will wind up getting lost...and you might not even realize it. But if you're wearing the correct prescription, you will begin to see, believe, and live in a way that not only helps you realize with clarity who you've been *made to be* and what you've been *made for*, but in a way that brings glory to God...which is ultimately what you and I have been created for!

I want to see things clearly. Here's the best news: we don't have to wait in line with 8 million other people and hope that we get to see someone who can give us the worldview glasses we need. God has given us the gift of His prescription in His Word.

It is said that David used the words he wrote in Psalm 119 to teach his young son Solomon the alphabet. But he used it for something more. He used it to shape Solomon's worldview. David writes, 'I will meditate on your precepts and fix my eyes on your ways' (Psalm 119:15). Why? David wanted Solomon to see things clearly. He says, 'Your word is a lamp to my feet and a light to my path' (Ps. 119:105).

The Christian worldview is rooted in the story of what God is doing in the world. God desires that your personal story will be a tiny chapter in His master story. And that's the next step we will take on our journey together as we look at culture and your place in the context of God's grand story!

Main Point

God desires that we develop a Christian worldview that shapes our beliefs and behaviors...all to His glory!

Questions for Reflection

• Choose a song from your current playlist. Watch the video and listen to the lyrics, paying careful attention to see and hear the worldview messages of the piece. How does the song answer the nine worldview questions mentioned in this chapter?

- Do you believe that music and media has shaped your worldview? Why or why not? If so, how?

- How has this chapter changed your thinking and perspective on the power of culture?

3. Culture, Your Story, and God's Story

You only live once. Carpe Diem. It's all about you. Find yourself. You be you. Just follow your heart.

Do any of these sayings sound familiar? They should. Each of these beliefs are elements in the cultural soup that we all swim in each and every day. Like we said earlier, soaking in the soup of our culture means that we come to believe what we see and hear in the soup, sometimes without us even knowing it. These beliefs then shape our worldview, which in turn guides our behaviors.

Think for a minute about the recent revelations about billionaire Jeffrey Epstein. Here's a guy who believed that life in this world was all about him. That belief was painfully evident in his behavior. He amassed great wealth and then used that money to live a lavish lifestyle that included indulging his own fantasies in ways that led to trafficking and using young girls to satisfy his own lustful desires. Absolutely sick and sinful! But not to Jeffrey Epstein. He followed his own sinful heart into crafting a personal story in which he was the main character, with nobody and nothing getting in the way of gratifying his own selfish wants. He was simply being true to his horribly sinful and skewed worldview. Of course, there are great lessons to be learned from the ending of Jeffrey Epstein's story, as he took his own life in the loneliness of a solitary prison cell.

We find it extremely disturbing that a man would choose to live this way. But if we aren't consciously careful, our story could be influenced by the same dominant self-centered ideas floating around in the cultural soup, and we could choose to live out a variation on the same theme. In today's world, the story the culture convinces us is right is the story that life is all about me, myself, and I. That's why more than one college and university these days jockeys for students by inviting them to choose them, as their campus is a place for you to come and 'Write your own story!' But is that the story for which we were created? Are we, in fact, to take control of our own lives and become the authors of our own story?

A self-centered story *isn't* the story God has created us to live. But we can so easily believe it, fall into it, and live it. The truth is, if that's the path we choose, we will ultimately die by it. Proverbs tells us, 'There is a way that seems right to a man, but its end is the way to death' (Proverbs 14:12).

WHAT STORY IS SHAPING YOU?

One of the great challenges you are facing now and which you will face for the rest of your life (Trust me! I know!) is the never-ending battle over which story you will choose to live. The philosopher Alasdair MacIntyre once wrote these words which help us understand what lies in the balance regarding our own personal story: *'I can only answer the question "What am I to do?" if I answer the prior question "Of what story or stories do I find myself a part?"'*[1]

The reality is that the God who made you, me, and everything else in this world is working out His story for all of His creation. And the good news is that by finding our place and part in God's story, we find the way that *is* right, ultimately leading to life and flourishing.

---

1   Alasdair MacIntyre, *After Virtue* (Notre Dame, IN: University of Notre Dame Press, 1984), p. 216.

What is this story? What is our place in it? How does this story shape our beliefs and behaviors? And how does knowing this story help us to develop a healthy view of culture?

GOD'S INCREDIBLE STORY!

Like many people, I for a long time had the wrong view of the Bible. I tended to think of the Bible as a rule book…filled with God's do's and don't's…with far more don't's than do's. But it was incredibly freeing when I discovered that the Bible was ultimately a revelation of God's four-chapter story, running from Genesis to Revelation with a seamless beauty that, when fully understood, was incredibly life-giving! Not only did this help me to see what *God* was up to in His world, but what He was calling *me* to be up to in my life. Knowing this story gives us a lens for looking at all reality. It is what shapes for us a biblical worldview that runs counter to culture. From this point forward, think about the Bible, your life, and culture in light of these four chapters in God's unfolding story.

GOD'S STORY CHAPTER 1—CREATION

I once heard someone say that the four most important words ever spoken are the first four words of the first book of the Bible: 'In

the beginning God...' It tells us that God is at
the center of all things and God is the creator
of all things. Everything in our lives must be
understood from this perspective, including
our own stories. The Creation account from
Genesis 1:1 to Genesis 2:25 tells us about God's
work over the course of the six days of creation,
and then His seventh day of rest.

While book after book has been written
about this first chapter in God's story, there are
three important points for you to grasp that are
important as we think about culture.

First, the Creation account tells us God's
plan for the world. What existed in the Garden
of Eden was a world that was complete, whole,
and without any kind of brokenness at all. It
was absolutely perfect in every possible way!
How could it be anything else? It was made by
our perfect God, and everything He made He
stamped with His declaration of 'Good!' There's
a Hebrew word to describe what existed in the
Garden of Eden: *Shalom.* We typically translate
this word as 'peace', which is correct, but it's
actually so much more. Shalom is a state of
universal flourishing, where everything exists
as God intended it to be. All of creation was

marked by a harmony. The Garden of Eden was a *culture* of perfection.

Second, the Creation account tells us who we are. God made human beings in His image. Nothing else in all of creation was made in God's image. And nothing else in all of creation received the stamp of approval God put on us after making us: '*Very* Good!' This is the proper starting place for my story and for your story. Our dignity, value, and identity are all rooted in our place as His image-bearers.

Third, the Creation account tells us what we are called as His image-bearers to do. God put us in the Garden with a task. He tells us to 'be fruitful and multiply', to 'fill the earth and subdue it', to have 'dominion' over everything on earth (Gen. 1:28), and to 'work' and 'keep' the rest of Creation (Gen. 2:15). In effect—and this is important—God has not only given us the gift of culture, but He commands us to create and make culture. This is all part of imaging God. We are co-creators, taking what He's created and making more out of it. Contrary to the popular belief of so many Christians, culture *is not* something to shun and run from. Rather, it is a good gift from God that He has given us to enjoy, use, care for, and develop. He desires and commands us to make something of the world! What results is human culture. God's command to our first parents, Adam and Eve, is a command for us today: 'Take what I've given you and advance it. Make culture that fits My design for Shalom in the world!'

GOD'S STORY CHAPTER 2—FALL

Life in our world is a mess. We experience disease, pain, emotional heartache, anxiety, stress, depression, relational breakdown, violence, racism, war, death...the list goes on and on. You know this to be true because you've experienced this in your life.

How did God's good creation that we read about in Chapter One of God's story suddenly get to be like this? The opening section of Genesis 3 tells us what happened.

It all begins with the enemy of God, Satan, who enters the Garden of Eden in the form of a serpent. Described as incredibly 'crafty' (Gen. 3:1), Satan's only desire is to wreck *everything* God has made and declared 'Good!' His mission was to knock over everything God had built. His strategy was to get our first parents to question God, asking the woman, 'Did God actually say, "You shall not eat of any tree in the garden?"' (Gen. 3:1).

'Did God actually say…?' Don't ever forget this truth: the wrecker of this world continues to use that strategy on us today. Satan then goes on to convince our first parents that disobedience to God's command would actually be freeing for them, as their eyes would be opened and they would become like God.

At the moment when our first parents eat of the forbidden fruit (Gen. 3:6), everything in Creation comes undone and nothing… NOTHING…is left the way it is supposed to be. We are broken. Our relationship with God is broken. We battle 24/7 with our own sinful nature. Culture becomes disordered and distorted by sin. The cultural soup is polluted. Our work becomes difficult and toilsome. We can no longer see clearly. And, there's nothing at all *we* can do about it.

But God…

GOD'S STORY CHAPTER 3—REDEMPTION

Let's be glad that God's story doesn't end with Chapter 2! God in His grace, mercy, and love very quickly intervenes on behalf of His creation. Without that intervention we are doomed. While all humanity will have to live with the consequences of sin and the ongoing efforts of the wrecker of this world, God reveals in Genesis 3:15 a grand and glorious plan to fix and re-do what sin has undone. He tells the serpent that He is going to send someone who will wreck him. And throughout the rest of the Bible, we see how God's rescue plan for all of creation unfolds through the incarnation, life, death, and resurrection of His Son, Jesus Christ. Redemption is the response of a loving God to a world that has been handcuffed by sin.

Jesus Christ, the Son of God, has come into the world to usher in God's Kingdom and to redeem individuals and all of creation from the bondage and curse of sin. And for those of us who are followers of Jesus, He has given us the responsibility to carry on the work of redemption in every nook and cranny of life. We are His representatives as we participate in God's work in the world, bringing light into the wrecker's darkness by *making and redeeming culture* on behalf of our King. We are to look back at God's Shalom, and then seek it and live it out today.

Now here's something very important you need to remember: Even though Jesus unlocks the handcuffs, the wrecker of this world is still on the move. Even though Satan was *defeated* at the cross, he is still *dangerous*. It's because of this that we are reminded to 'Be sober-minded; be watchful. Your adversary the devil prowls around like a roaring lion, looking for someone to devour' (1 Pet. 5:8). And how does Satan work to undo God's Shalom? By convincing us that the course of this world (broken culture) is a preferable map to the map of God's will and way.

GOD'S STORY CHAPTER 4—RESTORATION

Now, there's even more Good News! We know that Chapter 3 in God's story is not the end. Rather, it's a glorious *in-between* that looks forward with great anticipation to the final chapter in God's story, where we learn that God will make all things new!

The Book of Revelation, the last book in the Bible, tells us that a day is coming when God will usher in a never-ending new heaven and a new earth (Rev. 21:1-8). It will be a time when the lost Shalom that once existed in the Garden of Eden will return in an even more glorious form than it once existed! Heaven and earth will be restored. The wrecker of this world will be destroyed (Rev. 11:18) along with all tears, disease, brokenness, heartache...and even death itself. And here's something absolutely amazing: Chapter 4 will never end! Never! God's people will live with Him in eternal absolute Shalom! It is the ultimate 'happily ever after!'

WHAT NOW?

So...here we are. We live in this in-between time. Yes, Jesus has come into the world to usher in God's Kingdom. Yes, the Kingdom *is here*. But the Kingdom in its fullness *is still coming*. As we live in this in-between we are to recognize that yes, *'You only live once'*, so we must make the most of each moment and live to the glory of God as an act of worship rooted in our gratitude for what He has done for us through Jesus Christ. Yes, we are to live *Carpe Diem*, with each day intentionally seized to serve as Christ's hands and feet in the world. But rather than believing that *It's all about you,* we are to serve as signposts pointing away from ourselves and to the cross of Jesus Christ. Yes, we are all on that journey to *find yourself*, but we know that it's only in being found in Jesus Christ that we will flourish. The Creation narrative tells us what it means to be human. In essence, it's a new way to look at *You be you* as we come to embrace the identity, dignity, worth, and purpose given to us by God. And rather than choosing *Just follow your heart* as our personal mantra, we bury ourselves in God's Word in order to develop a biblical worldview through which we learn to follow God's heart for His creation, His will, and His way for our lives.

Scotty Smith reminds us, 'Even as Jesus is the main character in God's Story, each of us is freely invited to find our place in this grand narrative of hope. What a privilege, what an honor, what a calling…to live as a character in and a carrier of God's Story.'[2]

So how does knowing God's story shape the way we are to live in the now-but-not-yet Kingdom of God? How should a biblical worldview built on the foundation of God's story shape our stories? And, what does that mean for the way we are to engage in and with culture? That's the next step we will take on this journey.

Main Point

God's great plan for us is that we find and live our place in His grand story.

---

2   https://davidarms.com/gods-story/

Questions for Reflection

- How and where have you been encouraged to live your life in a self-centered story?

- What aspects of God's incredible four-chapter story do you find to be personally eye-opening and new? How does that change your understanding of your place in God's story?

- Satan—the wrecker of this world—endeavors to get us to question the truth of God's Word. Where are you most vulnerable to Satan's 'Did God really say…?' strategy?

4. Living Christianly in Culture

═══

I will never forget the five words of confession a high school senior shared with me as we walked together through the nasty fallout from a series of some very bad decisions he had made. He realized that he had stepped out of God's will and way as taught in the Bible. Simply stated, he had chosen to follow what the Apostle Paul calls 'the course of this world' (Eph. 2:2). In a split-second moment of decision he had turned his back on God and His Word, and allowed the messages of the cultural soup to shape his beliefs, his decisions, and his behaviors. Discouraged and broken, he held his head down in his hands as he said, 'I am very easily influenced.'

My friend is not alone. As followers of Jesus Christ, each of us is faced with an endless parade of choices regarding how to navigate life in today's culture. It's like walking a tightrope as we struggle to hear God's voice speak to us through His Word, while at the same time the loud and powerful voices of our culture scream guidance and direction in our ears. These influences are strong. We're all more easily influenced than we're willing to admit.

FINDING OUR PLACE IN GOD'S WORLD

How should we respond? Sometimes followers of Jesus just give up and give in, and they wind up following the lead of the culture. For example, think of the ways many professing followers of Jesus are wavering from God's order and design for marriage as it is clearly stated in Chapter 1 of God's story. God tells us that marriage is a covenantal, lifelong, monogamous relationship between one man and one woman. But in the church today, many are believing and living out ideas on marriage that reflect the culture's map rather than the map of God's Word.

Others decide that the best approach is to withdraw completely from the culture, assuming that any contact with the culture would leave them completely corrupt. They might even go so far as to believe that it is dangerous and wrong to establish friendships with people who aren't followers of Jesus.

Neither of these extremes are options for the follower of Jesus. Rather, there's a third way we are to follow that Jesus reveals to us when He prays on the night before His crucifixion.

What is this third way? In John 17:14-18 Jesus prays what is truly the will of God the Father with these words: 'I have given them your word, and the world has hated them because they are not of the world, just as I am not of the world. I do not ask that you take them out of the world, but that you keep them from the evil one. They are not of the world, just as I am not of the world. Sanctify them in the truth, your word is truth. As you sent me into the world, so I have sent them into the world.'

Re-read this prayer a couple of times to make sure you follow what Jesus is saying. Simply stated, Jesus calls us to keep our ears, hearts, and minds tuned in to His voice as revealed in the Bible. Then, with a commitment to hear and follow God's Word, we are to live *in* but not *of* the world.

You and I no longer belong to the world, but we *are* to continue to live in the world. As we live in the world, our charge is to be the hands and feet of Jesus—His presence—carrying on His kingdom-building mission.

As Jesus prays for us, it becomes clear that He wants us to infiltrate the culture, living in it as a transforming presence, while maintaining our distinct identity as His followers.

One theologian has helped me understand this by calling it a life of 'holy worldliness.' To be *holy* means to be separate and set apart in our love for and service to God. We are truly different because we are following His Word rather than the voices of the culture... voices that on most occasions would send us in another direction. Our lives are to be a 'true separation to God which is lived out in the world—the world which He made and sent His son to redeem.'[1]

BEING SALT AND LIGHT

In the Sermon on the Mount, Jesus used some metaphors that will help you understand how to live Christianly in the midst of today's culture.

First, Jesus tells us that we are to be 'the salt of the earth' (Matt. 5:13). Because they lived in a time without refrigerators, those who were listening knew that salt was used to preserve meat from decay. Salt was also used to bring

---

1   John Stott, *Christ The Controversialist* (Downers Grove, IL; InterVarsity Press, 1970), p. 191.

flavor and life to bland food, as it is today. When we live *in* but not *of* the world we represent Christ, serving as a transforming presence in the culture, bringing life where there is death, and seasoning where there is not flavor.

Second, Jesus tells us that we are to be 'the light of the world' (Matt. 5:14). We are to have a presence in the world so that the world can see us—in the midst of all the darkness in our culture—as we talk about and live out God's will and way.

In essence, what Jesus tells us about how to live is clearly related to how He teaches us to pray in what we call 'The Lord's Prayer' (Matt. 6:5-15). Whenever we recite the Lord's Prayer we say these words: 'Your kingdom come, your will be done, on earth as it is in heaven.' This is what it means to live *in* but not *of* the world! We are to represent Christ as His kingdom ambassadors, living out His kingdom priorities and agenda every minute of every day and in every area of life. The Apostle Paul reminds us of this when he tells us to no longer be conformed to this world, but to be conformed to God's Word (Rom. 12:1-2). We are to live counter-culturally.

THREE STEPS TO FAITHFUL LIVING

I've learned that there are some helpful steps to consciously take that help me to discern God's will and live counter-culturally in the midst of a confusing world that is changing so fast. These steps will not only help you see what's in the cultural soup as you swim in it, but respond in ways that bring honor and glory to God. Taking these steps are one way for you to, as Paul says, 'discern what is the will of God, what is good and acceptable and perfect' (Rom. 12:2).

Take some time to think about each of these steps. In the two chapters that follow, I will show you how taking these steps will help you navigate some specific culture issues (gender, and social media) that exist in your soup/world today. Think about each of these steps as combining in a process of going from *world,* to *Word,* to *walk.*

World

The first step is to ask *What's going on in the world?* Your task is to *discover* as much as you can about this particular element in the cultural soup. What is your culture saying about the way the world is? What is it saying about the way the world should be? What are the beliefs and values this cultural element wants me to believe and hold? How does this cultural element answer the worldview questions we looked at back in Chapter 2? How does this cultural element want me to serve the course of this world through my lifestyle and choices?

Word

The second step is one where you need to exercise the kind of discernment Paul speaks of in Romans 12:2. This is where you ask the question: *According to God's Word, what should be going on?* It is essential that you keep developing a growing knowledge of God's Word so that your skills in discernment are sharp. Keep going to God's Word to find an answer to this question. Go to trusted Godly friends and resources to help you find 'what is good and acceptable and perfect' (Rom. 12:2). *Discernment* is the practice of looking deeply at the cultural element to see if it represents those things God's Word says are good, true, right, and honorable...or, if it is representing and promoting those things God's Word says are evil, false, dishonorable, and wrong. You are putting the cultural element up against the measuring stick of God's Word to discern whether or not there is agreement or disagreement with God's never-changing truth (The Bible) and the Christian worldview.

Walk

The third step answers the question: *How should I respond?* It's decision time! This is the crucial and necessary step where you discover what it means to live a life of faithful obedience to God and His Word in the midst of our current world. If the cultural element lines up with the Christian worldview, we can celebrate it and affirm it. If not, we now need to think about how we will believe and live differently, counter-culturally, and to the glory of God. The great challenge comes when we see our calling to live God's Kingdom in opposition to a culture that is oftentimes promoting what the Bible calls the kingdoms of the world, the flesh, and the devil.

JESUS AND WORLD, WORD, AND WALK

One of the best models of living this way is found in Luke 4:1-13, where we read about Jesus being led by the Holy Spirit into the desert for forty days of ministry preparation. Take a minute to read Luke 4:1-13. Hungry from fasting, Jesus is tempted by the devil—

aka 'the ruler of this world' (John 14:30)—who wants to lead Jesus into falling away from His Kingdom-building mission and into serving the devil himself. In an effort to undo Jesus and wreck Him by keeping Him from doing His Father's will (just like the devil desires to do to us!), the devil tempts Jesus three times and in three ways. First, he tempts Jesus to turn stones into bread in order to misuse His divine power and satisfy His hunger apart from depending on God. Second, the devil promises Jesus all the kingdoms of the world if Jesus will only worship him rather than worshipping God. And finally, the devil tempts Jesus by misquoting Scripture and telling Jesus to test God's faithfulness to His promises.

Do you see what's happening here? The 'prince of this world' does everything he can to get Jesus to step out of the will of God and follow the lies. But in each of the three cases, Jesus sees what's going on, and He immediately responds by running to and 'walking' in the truths of God's Word!

World…Word…Walk. Are you willing to live a life of counter-cultural obedience to God and His Word? If so, let's now look at how this works out practically in the specific cultural soup of today's world.

Main Point

As followers of Jesus, we are called to live in, but not of the world.

Questions for Reflection

- In what ways have you seen Christians follow the map of culture rather than the map of God's Word?

- In what ways have you seen Christians withdraw from their culture? Are there times when our faith in Jesus requires us to withdraw from our culture?

- What are some good examples of 'holy worldliness' that you've seen?

5. World, Word, Walk on Gender

A teacher friend recently passed on a copy of a handwritten note that showed up on her high school campus. It was written by a former student who would have been in 10th grade had she not dropped out of school the year before. The girl had left the note in the school office and asked that it be passed on to a student who she hadn't seen in over a year. 'Could you give this to him?' she asked the school secretary. Her note included these words:

Hey Matt. I miss you. Do you remember me? Shelby Conner, but I go by Kyle now. I'm not transgender. I'm gender fluid. Sometimes I'm gender variant. I am also pansexual and polyamorous. How much have you changed? God, it's been so long since I've seen you.

Would you like to know just how quickly the cultural soup you're swimming in is changing?

Ask your parents to read Shelby's note. Watch the expression on their faces. Now, pick them up off the floor and ask them, 'What do you think of this?' Be ready to explain any terminology that is new to them (probably all of it!)...but familiar to you. If your parents are the least bit surprised or shocked, that's because a note like Shelby's was inconceivable back when they were in high school. The culture was much, much different in those old days.

GENDER CHANGES

When people ask me about the biggest youth culture shifts of the last ten years...or even five years, I don't even hesitate to mention the issue of *gender*. Beyond the terms Shelby used to describe herself—terms that are jaw-dropping for older people, but likely familiar to you—there is an ever-growing number of terms used to describe gender and sexual preferences. All of this is evidence of just how quickly the cultural soup is changing on one of the most foundational realities of human life, that is, how God has made us.

I'm guessing that most of you have been a part of a classroom experience where introductions include not only a person's name, but a list of their preferred pronouns.

Maybe you know a peer who has socially transitioned (changing name and pronouns), is presenting as something opposite of their birth gender (dressing differently), is on puberty blockers, has started cross-sex hormone therapy, or is planning on sex-reassignment surgery sometime in the future. Perhaps you are feeling some of these things in your own life as you navigate the difficult process of finding your way through the confusing maze of the adolescent years. And, maybe you are so in-tune with the current language regarding gender that I've actually irritated you here by using terms in ways that you would say are incorrect or even demeaning.

THINKING CHRISTIANLY ABOUT GENDER

What I want to invite you into is a short exercise in actually doing what we talked about in the last chapter, that is, looking at culture through the lens of a distinctively Christian worldview. It's an exercise in putting aside what we might already think and believe about gender, in order to discover what God thinks and says about gender. Specifically, I want to compare the world's story on gender, with God's story on gender so that we might gain a sense of how to live faithfully as followers of Jesus in God's world as we think about and live out gender.

Since the issue of gender is quite complex and getting more complex with each passing day, the process here will simply be a very short start that I would encourage you to continue with others who desire to live faithfully on this issue. So, continue the conversation with your parents, your youth workers, your pastor, and your Christian peers. Let's do this in the three categories we discussed—World, Word, and Walk.

GENDER: WHAT'S GOING ON IN THE *WORLD*?

As we stir up and look into today's cultural soup and what it has to say about gender, don't forget that in terms of God's story, God's good creation (Chapter 1) has been broken by humankind's sin (Chapter 2). Things are not the way they are supposed to be. While the culture *can* get the gender message right from time to time, the culture is sliding quickly into believing and living a gender message that gets it wrong.

Here are just a few of the gender messages that are pervasive in today's culture. Think about where you've seen and heard these beliefs expressed in media, conversations, your school, etc...and even how they've influenced your own beliefs.

• Your 'gender identity' is what you *feel* about yourself. You could *feel* like you are male, female, some combination of both, or actually neither. Your gender identity has nothing to do with the sex organs you were assigned at birth. Your gender *is not* biologically determined. What's in your pants or under your shirt does not tell you who or what you really are.

• To think of gender as falling into the binaries (only two opposite options) of male and female is completely wrong. There are no binaries. To think that there is only one or the other is wrong. In fact, there is a spectrum. Gender exists on a continuum. Some people might be more masculine. Some people might be more feminine. Some people move back and forth on the spectrum, feeling one way today and another way tomorrow. Some would identify as not even on the spectrum. All of this is normal!

• So, how do you discover your gender identity? That's entirely up to you! There is no other authority on your gender but you. You choose based on how you feel. Whatever you feel and think you are, you are! Nobody, even

God Himself, can tell you who or what you are. It's all a matter of your personal choice. Only you are sovereign over you!

• Your gender identity is at the foundation of *who* you are. It is your ultimate identity. Celebrate it. Live it out. You be you!

GENDER: WHAT SHOULD BE GOING ON ACCORDING TO GOD'S *WORD*?

As followers of Jesus, we must go to and trust God's Word as the spotlight that shines truth on our understanding of gender. Since the Bible is our authority, it communicates God's plan, purpose, will and way for how things are supposed to be. What does the Bible (God's story) tell us about God's plan, purpose, will and way for gender? Here are just a few basic starting points from Scripture. Think about how they differ from the world's story on gender.

• God has revealed His grand and glorious plan for humanity in the Creation account which is found in Genesis 1&2. If we want to know what it means to be human...to be *fully* human...we find that plan and purpose 'in the beginning.'

• Everything God created He pronounced as 'good!' But when He finished creating humans

He said 'very good!' And what He pronounced as very good was male and female…the binary genders He designed and assigned…male and female *only*, that are both fully human and equal in dignity. Our first parents, Adam and Eve, were given complementary biological forms and purposes so that they might work together to care for God's good creation, to be fruitful, and to multiply. God gave each of us anatomy and sex organs (and even genes in our DNA!) that tell us what gender we are, either male or female. This is the way things are supposed to be. Jesus affirms this in Matthew 19:4 when He says, 'Have you not read that he who created them from the beginning made them male and female?'

• Because of humankind's fall into sin, everything and everyone are broken. Just like he did with our first parents in the Garden of Eden, the wrecker of this world (Satan) comes to us desiring to keep us from understanding and pursuing things as they are supposed to be. Satan wants us to cooperate with him in the destruction of God's good order and design wherever that exists…including our understanding of gender. And just as he did in Genesis 3:1, Satan continues to get us to question, doubt, and turn from God's order and design by getting us to distrust God's authority. He deceives us, getting us to believe and live out lies so that all Creation and our own lives come undone. On gender and everything else he poses this doubt-inducing question: 'Did God really say…?' Ultimately, Satan will do anything he can to get us to join him in his rebellion against God.

• Our primary identity as followers of Jesus is not to be found in our gender. In fact, it should rest in nothing other than who we are as adopted and dearly loved sons and daughters of our Rescuer, Jesus Christ (Rom. 8:15-17).

GENDER: HOW SHOULD WE *WALK* FAITHFULLY IN OBEDIENCE TO GOD'S WORD IN TODAY'S WORLD?

As followers of Jesus Christ, we are called to live counter-culturally, which means that when it comes to gender, we will follow the will of God rather than the rapidly unfolding way of the world on gender. Here are some specific initial steps you can take to remain faithful to Christ and live to the Glory of God as you find yourself in Chapter 3 of God's story (Redemption).

• Never stop immersing yourself in God's Word. Study it. Run to it. Live in it. Engage with it when you are alone and when you are with your Christian friends. Remember, Satan will always work to derail you from hearing God's voice so that you might listen to and believe the 24/7 onslaught of the voices in the cultural soup that lull us into embracing 'the course of this world.' Remember, whenever you find yourself asking the question, 'Did God really say…?', run…RUN!…to God's Word to remind yourself of what God has *really* said.

• Continually ask God to root and grow your identity in who you are in Jesus Christ and in Jesus Christ alone.

• Never allow your feelings to dictate and misshape your understanding of truth. The world wants you to 'follow your heart' on all matters, including gender. I tell people all the time that if I were to follow my heart I would be in prison. Yep, my heart is that broken. Yours is too. Jeremiah 17:9 tells us that 'the heart is deceitful above all things, and desperately sick.' Recognize that even though you are a child of God, you still have to battle your sinful nature. Take some time to read about the Apostle Paul's struggle with sin in Romans 7. Yes, our struggle to know and do what's right is real. But Paul reminds us that Jesus Christ delivers us from sin! (Rom. 7:24-25). We have great hope. Judge your feelings by Scripture, rather than judging Scripture by your feelings.

• If you are currently struggling to navigate issues of your gender, don't despair. You are not alone...either in your experience or in your effort to navigate your feelings and confusion. God is not calling you to walk through this alone. Go to a trusted Christian adult (parent, youth worker, pastor, etc) who will not only listen to you, pray for you, and walk with you, but who can connect you with a qualified Christian counselor who can help you get answers to your questions on gender and walk with you through your struggle.

• Even if you are not struggling with gender issues yourself, you no doubt will be given many opportunities to be the hands and feet of Jesus to those who are struggling with gender. Jesus gives us a clear example of how to engage with those who adopt worldly ideas and practices about gender. In John 8:1-22 He encounters the woman caught in adultery. His interaction with her is marked by a perfect balance of grace and truth. He does not condemn her to death. He shows her grace. And, He loves her enough to tell her the truth.

Her actions have been wrong and she needs to go and sin no more. Our friends struggling with gender issues need us to lovingly show that same balance of grace and truth.

While we've just scratched the surface here on world, word, and walk, use these steps to go more deeply into understanding and addressing the issues related to gender...issues that are unfolding all around us in today's culture. You will be bringing great Biblical light into deep cultural darkness.

Main Point

God in His goodness has created and given us each our gender, which is indicated by our anatomy, either male or female.

Questions for Reflection

- What beliefs do you hold regarding gender? Based on what you've read in this chapter, are your beliefs more reflective of the culture's map on gender, or God's map for gender?

- What movies, music, TV, books, and advertising have you encountered that are shaping people's views on gender these days?

- How would you communicate God's message on gender to a friend who is questioning their own gender identity?

6. World, Word, and Walk on Social Media

I was recently scrolling through the thousands of photos I've taken on my smartphone when I got to thinking about cameras. I went to Google to find out when the first photograph was taken. I was surprised to learn that it was way back in 1816. My search went even further and I learned that an interesting conversation about photos was recorded in a newspaper story a few decades later, in 1895. It seems that a newspaper photographer had taken a picture of a person and the person asked to see it. It was unusual to have even one photo of yourself back in those days. Shocked by what he saw of himself in the photo, the man asked, 'Good Lord! Do I look like that?' The photographer replied, 'The camera does not lie.'

I DON'T MEASURE UP

The camera does not lie? Or does it? Or, is it more accurate to assume in today's world of social media where we take and share photo after photo, that it's not the camera that lies, but rather those of us who filter, manipulate, and photoshop our photos before we put them out there for the world to see. Each of us knows this to be true, as all of us have looked at a post from someone we know and seen an online representation (photos or text) that looks and sounds nothing like their offline reality. If you're like me, you have probably even misrepresented yourself. We're horrified when someone tags us or shares a photo where we just don't look good…and we let them know it, don't we! 'DELETE THAT NOW!'

Why do we do this? The simple answer is this: the cultural soup that we swim in each and every day has set standards for image and identity that are so high that none of us can ever measure up. So, through the use of apps, digital tools, and flat-out lies, we are able to 'fix' our perceived shortcomings, and then hope that our post will serve not to represent us as we know that *we really are*, but as *we think we should be*. 'Look at me! Like me!' is what we seem to always be saying even though we might never use words. And then, we get locked into that anxiety-inducing and destructive habit of comparing ourselves to others. When we start to compare we see that we fail, because there's always someone who looks better. Teddy Roosevelt once said that 'comparison is the thief of joy.' Thanks to social media and the pressure we all feel to look and seem perfect, comparison might also be the thief of honesty. We fail to be honest about ourselves to others. We even fail to be honest about ourselves *to ourselves* as we start to believe the lies that we're ugly, imperfect, and ultimately 'less than' everybody else. Have you ever felt that way? You're not alone.

THINKING CHRISTIANLY ABOUT SOCIAL MEDIA

I believe that social media and technology are good gifts from God. But like all other good gifts from God, we need to think seriously about how the Bible and our faith should shape the way that we use social media and technology. We can use these gifts in ways that lead to our undoing and destruction, or we can use them to advance our human flourishing as we enlist them as tools to worship and glorify God.

I've found that if we allow ourselves to get caught up in how the cultural soup tells us to use social media and technology, we're prone to anxiety, stress, depression, time-wasting, comparison, loneliness, jealousy, body dysmorphia, competitiveness, arrogance, addiction, relational breakdown, self-centeredness, insecurity, and ultimately the idolatry of working to put ourselves at the center of the universe. Not only does research confirm this, but your own experience, I'm sure, shows this to be true.

In addition to all the benefits of God's good gift of technology and social media, there are many ways that technology and social media can undo us...far too many to talk about here. But two of the biggest ways that social media is undoing all of us—teenagers and adults alike— are (1) how social media so easily becomes a time waster for both those who post and those who are consumed with reading posts, and (2) how social media is uniquely suited, if we aren't careful, to become a playground where we can indulge our sinful natures in ways that lead to glorification of ourselves rather than glorification of God.

What would happen if we looked at social media, our smartphone use, how we use our online time, and what we post, through the lens of a distinctively Christian worldview? How would our habits change? Could we find freedom and healing from the negative effects of social media on our lives? I believe we can, but it will take an investment of your thought, your effort, and a heavy dose of your self-discipline. Remember, being a follower of Jesus Christ is not an easy path.

Let's compare the world's story on social media with God's story on social media. Let's work together to gain a sense of how to live faithfully as followers of Jesus Christ as we use the good gift of our smartphones and other devices. Again, our look here will be short and not complete. But I hope it will serve to start you on the journey of thinking more deeply about these things as you converse with your parents, your youth workers, your pastor, and your Christian peers about social media.

SOCIAL MEDIA: WHAT'S GOING ON IN THE *WORLD*?

Here are just a few of the dangerous and destructive ways that our culture encourages us to understand and use social media:

• 'It's all about you!' Since you are the center of your universe your life is ultimately about pursuing self-fulfillment and personal happiness, nothing else. Your feelings will tell you who you *really* are. Then, you should focus your life on expressing the authentic 'you' to the world. You are entitled to seek the praise and admiration of others. As your following grows, so will your value and worth!

• Social media is the perfect platform to use to reveal your desired self to the world. This is where you make, re-make, express, and promote who you want the world to see you to be. Post, post, and post.

• You are a 'brand' to sell to the world on social media. You need to advance yourself through carefully curating and promoting a persona that will win you likes, followers, friends, and status in the online world. The ultimate success will come as you climb the ladder and become an influencer of others, maybe even a celebrity whose presence is so strong, that you can make a few bucks...or much more than just a few bucks...as a sponsored endorser of products. If others get in the way of success, don't hesitate to step on them or over them. Remember, it's all about you!

• Do whatever it takes to re-make and re-package yourself in order to advance yourself. If your achievements, real or made-up, will catch the attention of others, then put them out there. *Show* through photos and *tell* through your posts. If you can grab attention through posting about your anxiety and depression—real or made-up—go for it. 'Be' whatever works.

• Your value and worth hinge on what others think of you. Carefully study how influencers present themselves. Then, copy it. Study their photos. Pose, filter, photoshop…whatever it takes in terms of time and effort to get the photo that presents you not so much in *your* best light, but in the best light of cultural expectations and standards. Dress up. Dress down. Whatever it takes. Reinvent yourself however and whenever necessary to keep all eyes on you.

• Expect to be anxious and depressed as a small price to pay for developing your following. Of course, when your 'authentic self' isn't good enough, your anxiety will increase. Relief will come as a result of working harder and harder to present yourself to the world in whatever image finally clicks. Keep striving to perfect your performance.

SOCIAL MEDIA: WHAT SHOULD BE GOING ON ACCORDING TO GOD'S *WORD*?

You won't find any direct references to the use of 21st century technology, smartphones, and social media in God's Word. But as you search the Bible from cover-to-cover you will find consistent guidance and principles for life in God's world that you can apply to counter the cultural message on how to use social media. The Bible offers guidance on how to be a faithful 'digital disciple' of Jesus Christ.

• God is God. You are not. Our first parents, Adam and Eve, fell into sin as a result of giving in to the temptation to take control of their own lives and become like God (Gen. 3:1-7). They bought that lie that we still fall victim to: 'It's all about you!' Ever since, human beings have been bent toward taking the place of God, seeking to *be worshipped* rather than *to worship*. When God gave His people the Ten Commandments, He established His rightful place as their God, commanded them to place no other gods before Him, and commanded them to never make or bow down to idols. The Scriptures from start to finish remind us of our default setting to forget God and put ourselves first. However, it's not and never should be about you.

• Everything we are, everything we do, everything we say...it's all an act of worship because it is directed toward giving glory to someone or something. Social media is a perfect place to seek glory for yourself. But the Apostle Paul reminds us in 1 Corinthians 11:31 that 'whatever' we do—which includes our use of social media—is to be done 'to the glory of God.' We have been made by God for worship, and worship we will—either God or something we turn into a god—every minute of every day. But when we live in the way God designed us by seeking to worship only Him, we find amazing freedom!

• Seeking to find your identity in anything other than who you are as someone created by God in the image of God, and adopted by God into His family as a son or daughter through your union with Jesus Christ, *is absolutely futile*. It will undo you and destroy you. Your performance, online or anywhere else, does not matter. Not what you look like, what you achieve, nor the number of likes and followers. Peace, freedom from anxiety, and purpose will only come when you rest your identity in who you are as a beloved child of God through the work of Jesus Christ.

• God values and commands honesty. When we are dishonest through our online portrayals, we are actually engaged in telling lies. The Ten Commandments tell us, 'You shall not bear false witness against your neighbor' (Exod. 20:16). God demands that His followers be truthful and honest. No half-truths. No exaggerations. No attempts to shield our true selves from others. No manipulated selfies. Any attempt to tweak the truth and deceive others is wrong. The beauty of this lies in the fact that we find freedom in telling the truth about ourselves, as we allow ourselves to be truly known rather than expending time and anxious energy to keep ourselves masked!

• Time is a gift from God. We've only been given so much…24 hours in each day. We are to steward the gift of our time just like we do everything else…to the glory of God! Time is not to be wasted, but invested in doing God's Kingdom work. Remember, we are living now in Chapter 3 of God's Story. Our place in this world is to represent Christ by engaging in the work of advancing His Kingdom priorities. The Apostle Paul tells us that we are to 'look carefully how you walk, not as unwise but as wise, making the best use of the time, because the days are evil. Therefore, do not be foolish, but understand what the will of the Lord is' (Eph. 5:15-17). It is not wrong to use social media. But it is wrong to use it in ways that waste time.

• In a world where we are prone to selfishly step on and over others, God requires us to live differently by loving and serving our neighbor. 'Do nothing from selfish ambition or conceit, but in humility count others more significant than yourselves' (Phil. 2:3).

SOCIAL MEDIA: HOW SHOULD WE *WALK* FAITHFULLY IN OBEDIENCE TO GOD'S WORD IN TODAY'S WORLD?

The Social Media battle has been one I've had to fight personally since the day I went on the internet, and even more-so in the days since my smartphone has allowed me to carry around social media 24/7. I've had to navigate all the dangers I've mentioned so far, and more. What's been most helpful to me is to build some personal borders and boundaries when it comes to social media. While I am far from consistently hitting the mark (yep, still), I endeavor to follow the wisdom of Proverbs whenever I'm using social media. In Proverbs we read these wise words: 'Do you see a man who is hasty in his words? There is more hope for a fool than for him' (Prov. 29:20), and 'When words are many, sin is not absent, but he who holds his tongue is wise' (Prov. 10:19).

Here are some steps I've adopted and found helpful as I have learned to take 'a purposeful pause' before ever hitting 'send', 'post', 'tweet', 'like', or 'reply.'

First, decide whether or not to post.

A man named Alan Jacobs is particularly helpful here. Jacobs suggests we adopt eight standards/guidelines as we are thinking about posting on social media. These guidelines have really helped me to stay out of trouble over the years!

• I don't have to say something just because everyone around me is.

• I don't have to speak about things I know little or nothing about.

• I don't have to speak about issues that will be totally forgotten in a few weeks or months by the people who at this moment are most strenuously demanding a response.

• I don't have to spend my time in environments that press me to speak without knowledge.

• If I can bring to an issue heat, but no light, it is probably best that I remain silent.

• Private communication can be more valuable than public.

• Delayed communication, made when people have had time to think and calm their emotions, is almost always more valuable than immediate reaction.

• Some conversations are more meaningful and effective in living rooms (school cafeterias) or at dinner tables, than in the middle of main street.[1]

Second, decide *what* to post.

I've adopted a filter of several successive questions through which I take time to allow my potential posts to pass. You'd be surprised how much time, effort, and social media noise you could save by eliminating posts, by pausing to ask yourself these questions!

1. Does this matter? If the answer is 'no', don't post it.

2. Is this a faithful and truthful representation of me (my family, my life, etc.)? Or, is it a fabricated lie? Only post the truth. Ditch the lies.

3. Is this useful to others? Or, am I wasting other people's time? It's bad enough that I struggle with wasting my own time. I don't need to help other people waste theirs!

---

1   https://www.theamericanconservative.com/jacobs/im-thinking-it-over/

4. Does this promote and reflect Kingdom of God living and human flourishing? If it advances God's kingdom agenda to recover Shalom, by all means, post it!

5. Does this promote and reflect the kingdoms of the world, the flesh, and the devil and undermine human flourishing? If this helps the wrecker of this world to wreck it even more, well, walk away from it.

6. Does this glorify God? Or does this glorify me? You know what to do here!

Finally, establish your own posting parameters.

I've adopted the following standards for what I post on social media. These guidelines have served me well, allowing me to gain time and refocus my mind on what really matters, while helping me to develop the habit of pushing back on what my sinful self would love for me to do on social media. Perhaps you'll find them helpful too. And, take the time to add your own parameters to these. They are quite counter-cultural, I know. But isn't that how we're called to live as followers of Christ?

• Don't post about me. I know this goes against what most everyone is doing online. But this has helped me steer away from indulging in the idolatry of self.

• Post to inform. I want to let people know about events, stories, articles, devotions, etc. that they will find helpful, but which they might not already know about.

• Post to educate. I want to help others grow in their faith and knowledge. I look for things to pass on to them that will equip them to grow in their faith.

• Post to encourage. As you know, life is tough. So many of our friends are anxious, depressed, discouraged, and feeling broken. The online world typically serves to only magnify those experiences. I look for ways to build others up through my posts or comments. A word of warning: don't offer up likes and positive comments on posts that seek affirmation for the wrong things. An easy example: selfies that are nothing but attempts to get likes based on finding my identity and value in my appearance.

• Only post humor that is appropriate. I love funny stuff. But it's way too easy to share humor that is demeaning to others or crude in nature. Keep it clean! And don't use humor that tears down individuals or groups of people.

Social media and technology are a good gift from God. Don't ditch your technology. Rather, learn to use it as a tool to advance God's Kingdom. You're probably going to have it for the rest of your life. Remember that how you use it is always an act of worship in one direction or another.

Main Point

We need to live counter-culturally on social media, making it a place where we worship and glorify God rather than a place where we worship and glorify ourselves.

Questions for Reflection

- How much time do you spend every day, on average, engaged with your smartphone? Would you say that your smartphone habits are healthy or unhealthy? Why?

- What influence do you believe social media has had on your own life? Is that influence positive or negative?

- How can you shift your habits in order to glorify and worship God through your social media use?

Conclusion

The words 'Follow me' are spoken by Jesus 22 times in the Gospels. They sit at the core of what it means to find one's created purpose in life as we enter into a lifelong relationship with God through His Son, Jesus Christ. Ultimately, we all must respond in one way or another to this invitation. When we respond with a 'Yes!' to Jesus, we are choosing to follow the map of His will and way as He reveals His map for our lives in the Bible. We are also saying that we will try to become so aware of the map for living that we marinate in as inhabitants of culture, that we will only celebrate and affirm the cultural map where it affirms God's will and way. Likewise, we will endeavor, with God's help, to make decisions to steer away from the map of the culture where it leads us astray.

In Matthew 4:19, we learn that when Jesus issued this command to Peter, Andrew, James, and John, they *immediately* left all that they were doing to follow Jesus. In Mark 10:21, the response of the rich young ruler was the exact opposite. We read that he was 'disheartened' by this command which warrants a change of allegiance...he continued to listen to the voices of his culture that defined what's most valuable in life...and 'he went away sorrowful.'

May we follow in the footsteps of the disciples as they followed in the footsteps of Jesus by answering *immediately* in the affirmative to Jesus' command. Still, they were a bunch of broken and imperfect people who often struggled to hear and follow God's voice, yet that was their lifelong endeavor. They learned, as we can, that a lifetime of listening to Jesus and His Word is life-giving and leads to human flourishing.

May God bless you with ears, eyes, and a heart focused on seeing, hearing, and following His will and way!

Appendix A: What Now?

- What was the last movie you watched? Go back and view it again. This time, go beyond viewing as entertainment, and engage with the movie from a posture of critique. What are the worldview messages depicted and promoted in the film?

- Look over your current music playlist. Choose one or two songs to evaluate through the process of World-Word-Walk.

- Find a person over the age of sixty and ask to have a conversation about culture. Have them describe what the youth culture was like when they were your age. What's different? What's the same? What do they love about today's youth culture? What concerns them about today's youth culture?

- Ask your parents to share their greatest concerns about today's youth culture.

Ask them to share their wisdom on Godly decision-making.

- Start a viewing/listening group that meets regularly to evaluate a film, book, music, video game, etc. that's popular in today's youth culture.

- Take a week and log how you use your time. At the end of the week, go back and evaluate whether your time is being spent in a balanced or imbalanced way.

- Establish a daily time to focus on reading and studying God's Word.

- Adjust your schedule to spend less time focused on social media and more time focused on real flesh-and-blood human interaction.

Appendix B: Other Books on this Topic

Plantinga, Cornelius, *Engaging God's World: A Christian Vision of Faith, Learning, and Living* (Eerdmans, 2002).

Perritt, John, *A Student's Guide to Technology* (Christian Focus, 2020).

Hatton, Kristen, *Facetime: Your Identity In A Selfie World* (New Growth Press, 2017).

Sire, James, *The Universe Next Door: A Basic Worldview Catalog* (InterVarsity Press, 2020).

Seagraves, Brian & Leavine, Hunter, *Gender: A Conversation Guide for Parents and Pastors* (The Good Book Company, 2018).

Keller, Timothy, *Counterfeit Gods*, (Penguin Books, 2011).

Stott, John, *The Radical Disciple: Some Neglected Aspects of Our Calling*, (IVP Books, 2014).

Keller, Timothy, *God's Wisdom for Navigating Life,* (Viking, 2017).

Mueller, Walt, *How To Use Your Head To Guard Your Heart: A 3(D) Guide To Making Wise Media Choices* (available online at www.cpyu.org).

Reformed Youth Ministries (RYM) exists to reach students for Christ and equip them to serve. Passing the faith on to the next generation has been RYM's passion since it began. In 1972 three youth workers who shared a passion for biblical teaching to youth surveyed the landscape of youth ministry conferences. What they found was an emphasis on fun and games, not God's Word. Therefore, they started a conference that focused on the preaching and teaching of God's Word. Over the years RYM has grown beyond conferences into three areas of ministry: conferences, training, and resources.

- **Conferences:** RYM's youth conferences take place in the summer at a variety of locations across the United States and are continuing to expand. We also host parenting conferences throughout the year at local churches.

- **Training:** RYM launched an annual Youth Leader Training (YLT) conference in 2008. YLT has grown steadily through the years and is offered in multiple locations. RYM also offers a Church Internship Program in partnering local churches as well as youth leader coaching and youth ministry consulting.

- **Resources:** RYM offers a variety of resources for leaders, parents, and students. Several Bible studies are offered as free downloads with more titles regularly being added to their catalogue. RYM hosts multiple podcasts: *Parenting Today*, *The Local Youth Worker*, and *The RYM Student Podcast*, all of which can be downloaded on multiple formats. There are many additional ministry tools available for download on the website.

If you are passionate for passing the faith on to the next generation, please visit www.rym.org to learn more about Reformed Youth Ministries. If you are interested in partnering with us in ministry, please visit www.rym.org/donate.